things
i've
learned
about
loss

things
i've
learned
about
loss

Dana Shields

CHRONICLE BOOKS

SAN FRANCISCO

Library of Congress Cataloging-in-Publication Data

Names: Shields, Dana, author.
Title: Things I've learned about loss / Dana Shields.
Other titles: Things I have learned about loss
Description: San Francisco : Chronicle Books, [2020].
Identifiers: LCCN 2019051684 | ISBN 9781452181066 (hardcover)
Subjects: LCSH: Bereavement. | Consolation. | Conduct of life.
Classification: LCC BF575.G7 S475 2020 | DDC 155.9/37—dc23
LC record available at https://lccn.loc.gov/2019051684

Manufactured in China.

Design by Rachel Harrell.

10 9 8 7 6 5 4 3 2 1

Chronicle books and gifts are available at special quantity
discounts to corporations, professional associations, literacy
programs, and other organizations. For details and discount
information, please contact our premiums department at
corporatesales@chroniclebooks.com or at 1-800-759-0190.

Chronicle Books LLC
680 Second Street
San Francisco, California 94107
www.chroniclebooks.com

For Mom and Dad, in honor of Jeb.

Jeb was the first Shields family member killed while on active duty in the US Armed Forces since the Civil War.

———

Contents

—

Introduction

On March 21, 1991, at 7 a.m., I heard my local radio announce that there had been a midair collision between two US Navy P-3 Orion airplanes from Moffett Field in California. My little brother, Jeb, was a naval officer at Moffett. I immediately called Jeb at home and left a message on his voicemail, "Hi Jeb, I heard about the crash. I hope you weren't on one of the planes. Call me."

I waited for his call all day long. I couldn't focus on work. I called Jeb's boss at Moffett Field every hour to see if Jeb had been on one of the planes involved in the crash. Finally, in the late afternoon, Jeb's boss informed me that yes, Jeb had been on one of the planes.

Shock is so weird. I felt numb. I felt like a zombie. Everyone around me seemed normal, but my world was in slow motion. It was surreal. I felt like a ghost, slowly floating through my own life. I remember going to the bank and staring at the bank teller. Just staring. And not knowing what to say. She kept asking if I was alright. Eventually, I think I told her, "My little brother is dead."

Ten years later, 9/11 occurred. One of the people on the airplanes was a family friend.

To help his parents and siblings get through their tragedy, I wrote them a letter about my experience after losing Jeb and everything I had learned about the process of grieving. It turned into an intimate little folding book, in which the spectrum of emotions experienced during the grieving process was also visually expressed through a spectrum of colors as the book moved from cool blues and purples to angry reds and oranges and, finally, to hopeful greens and yellows. I made several of these tiny books by hand and sent one to each of his family members, along with a tree sapling for them to plant in his memory.

A year later, two more friends lost their husbands, so I sent each of them a copy of my tiny book and a tree sapling. Then their friends who were dealing with loss began asking for my little books. Then their friends' friends. I wanted to comfort each of them and let them know that they were not alone, whether they had lost someone to an accident, old age, disease, birth, miscarriage, illness, cancer, suicide, or addiction. I wanted to help them through the painful process of healing. I wanted to let them know that my little book and I were there for them. I wanted them to know that however they felt, it was probably normal. That even if the way they were grieving felt scary, it was probably OK. And that counseling would help; counseling would help them heal faster and make sense of it all. It helped me. Without it, I couldn't have written this book.

This book is a big hug from me to the hearts of those who ache with grief. You are not alone. It's a process we all have to go through in order to come out the other side. It will take time, and maybe asking for help, but it will get better. You will eventually feel hopeful again. And while your life may never be the way it used to be, that will be OK too.

I hope that this book is a comfort to you.

This little book
is a hug, from
me to you

Stages of grief

I've learned there are different stages of grief. Here are some of them:

shock

sadness

anger

guilt

acceptance

hope

These stages are different for every person and every situation. Sometimes all the stages happen in an hour; sometimes it takes months or years. And they may not all happen. They may not go in order, last equal amounts of time, or have obvious beginnings and endings. Grieving is a strange and confusing process for everyone. It just is.

Shock

It was a sunny spring afternoon when I learned about Jeb's accident. After I hung up the phone, I felt like I was in a trance. I had just experienced a horrible tragedy. A catastrophe. My heart was imploding. But when I looked around, everything looked normal. The people walking around me, happily chatting in downtown Palo Alto, had no idea that my brother had just died with twenty-six other young men in a horrific plane crash. Their lives were busy. Mine had suddenly stopped. One minute Jeb was flying in an airplane, the next he didn't exist. It was surreal. I just could not believe it. I felt so alone. Lost. Numb.

The next few weeks were a bizarre blur. All I knew was that something had suddenly forever changed. I remember hearing Jeb's name called at the Navy's memorial service and thinking to myself, *Why are they calling Jeb's name? Why are there Navy airplanes flying over the ceremony?* My brain just couldn't accept the truth all at once. It took between three and six months for it to slowly sink in that he wasn't coming back.

I've learned these are normal reactions. These feelings of shock, numbness, and incredulity are likely familiar to everyone who has lost someone, whether or not that death was sudden. Maybe our brains know to only feed us a little bit of trauma at a time. Otherwise, the shock of it all at once might be too heartbreaking to withstand.

Nightmares

I had absolutely terrifying nightmares during the first few months after the accident. Gruesome. I'd wake up screaming so loudly that I'd scare my roommates and neighbors awake.

I've learned my nightmares were caused by post-traumatic stress disorder (PTSD) and nightmares are common when grieving a disturbing or unexpected loss. With help from counseling, they eventually went away. I can't say enough about getting help from professionals.

Unsure how to act

———

I felt so unsure of how to act. I attended three Navy memorial services for my brother. The last was near my parents' home in Maine. The service in Maine happened on a dismal, cold, and wet day. After the service, guests came over to my parents' house.

No one really knew what we should be saying or doing. My dad asked me if we should entertain our guests by turning on the Final Four basketball game. Would it be disrespectful or a welcome relief? What would Jeb want us to do? We decided Jeb would have wanted us to have fun and watch the game, so we turned it on. But no one really watched. It was a little awkward.

I've learned going outside for a walk is incredibly helpful and healing. When it stopped raining, I asked if anyone wanted to go for a walk. Surprisingly, everyone came. We walked down the narrow country road near my parents' house like a small parade, past the weathered three-hundred-year-old barns, farmhouses, and rock walls. It was so much better than sitting uncomfortably inside. It felt good to breathe fresh air, and we didn't even need to talk if we didn't feel like it. I highly recommend it.

Sadness

There were a lot of incredibly sad days at first. I hated having to pretend that everything was fine and fake a smile even when I didn't feel like it. It was distressing when people I didn't know well wanted to have a conversation in the neighborhood or grocery store checkout line. I remember wishing I could tell them the truth: *My little brother just died.* But I didn't say that. I didn't know what to say. Instead, I just nodded and smiled weakly.

I've learned feeling sad, depressed, and lonely is normal. My sadness and pain would come and go. Sometimes it was as if nothing had ever happened. Sometimes I wondered how and why I should go on living. I remember feeling empty. Alone. Dead inside. My brain was numb. I couldn't think.

Nothing really mattered, not even my favorite things. Nothing brought me joy. Food in the fridge looked inedible, music seemed annoying, and I was a mess. I lived in my pj's and couldn't be bothered with a shower. I didn't care about anything. I wanted to fall asleep and never wake up.

Through therapy, I've learned these distressing feelings are normal. I finally asked for help, and I am so glad I did. *Please* don't be afraid to ask for help if you are struggling.

Anxiety

I've learned it's normal to feel especially unsettled before certain dates. For me, those were Christmas, Jeb's birthday, and the day of his accident. Sometimes anxiety would happen a week or so before, sometimes the day of. I'd suddenly feel irritable or anxious and unable to make basic decisions, unsure whether I wanted to go on a walk or not. I'd start on a walk. Then stop. Then start. Then turn around. Finally, I'd begin to sob.

I realized crying was what I needed to do the whole time. I think our brains (and hearts) need the release.

Crying

I've learned crying is a good thing. Sometimes I needed to cry but couldn't. My pain felt like an ominous thunderstorm building in pressure and intensity, getting closer and closer, except my storm cloud would never burst. I had to experiment with different ways to make myself cry. I would force myself to go on a long run or beat my pillow against my bed over and over until I started sobbing.

Crying seemed to cleanse my exhausted mind. After crying, I felt peaceful and slept soundly. Maybe all the energy I was unconsciously using to keep my feelings inside was finally released when I cried.

Everyone is different, and I hope you can find what helps you cry. When the tears come, let them flow. Stop what you're doing, pull over the car, and just cry. It is important to let it all out so you can heal.

Sleep

I've learned sleep can be inconsistent. Sometimes I slept a lot. Sometimes I didn't sleep at all. I was amazed at how much energy it took to keep my sadness inside. I felt tired all the time.

I've learned it's normal to feel exhausted, that it takes a lot of physical energy for one's heart and mind to mend. So sleep. It feels good. Sleep. Sleep. Sleep.

Visits

Not even a week after he died, I could have sworn Jeb was in the back seat of my car. I was a little scared, but oddly comforted. *Maybe he had come to say goodbye?* In the month following the crash, I kept feeling his presence. Quite often, I would be startled in the middle of the night by a dream of Jeb as a little boy, standing next to my bed, quietly watching me sleep. Then I would wake up and open my eyes, but I would still see him for a few seconds before he disappeared.

I've learned "visits" are a very common and (hopefully) comforting phenomenon.

Anger

I've learned feeling angry and resentful is normal. I was furious. *Whose fault was this? Who could I blame? It could have been prevented!*

I've learned to let the anger out. It felt good to stamp my feet in puddles and get my legs absolutely plastered with mud while on my walks. Pillows were helpful too. My therapist suggested I smash my pillow against my bed as hard as I could, over and over again, and then bury my face in it and scream. It worked. I recommend it.

Sometimes I would completely fall apart. Once, I let my anger and frustration about Jeb's death build up so much that I slammed a plate of spaghetti down on the counter—over and over and over until it broke into a million little pieces.

I've learned, when you're grieving, it's not uncommon to have intense emotional reactions. But try not to break anything. It's much better to use your pillow as a punching bag.

Guilt

I used to feel guilty for begging Jeb to choose to be stationed in California instead of Hawaii. If Jeb had picked Hawaii, he would probably still be alive. But I had selfishly wanted him to be near me so we could go running, hiking, and skiing, and spend holidays together.

I've learned it's normal to feel guilty. I shouldn't have blamed myself for things I said or did before Jeb died. With time and counseling, I was able to find peace. Give yourself some grace.

Acceptance

Acceptance happens over time. It doesn't mean you are no longer sad. It doesn't mean your grieving is over. It just means you are healing, little by little. You are facing your pain and learning how to live with it.

First anniversary

On the very first anniversary of the accident, several of the grieving families and I rented a boat and sailed a few miles out to sea off the coast of San Diego. Somewhere near the area where our boys died, we turned off the boat's engine and just sat quietly, staring at the soft blue-green swells. I leaned over the side of the boat and filled a mason jar with seawater because I wanted to bring Jeb home with me. We threw wreaths of flowers. They bobbed like beautiful little life rafts.

I knew I was as close as I would ever get to being near Jeb again. I really wanted to say goodbye, apologize for things I had said, and tell him how much I loved and missed him. So I wrote him a letter, put it in a bottle, and threw it in.

I've learned being able to say "goodbye" and "I'm sorry" is enormously healing. In retrospect, it was a turning point in my grieving process.

Belongings

I've learned not to give belongings away until I'm ready. I found comfort in wearing his clothes. I put most of his things in a box in the attic until, years later, I could look at them. Occasionally, I'd unexpectedly stumble onto one of his belongings, which would break my heart all over again.

It can be incredibly difficult to part with a loved one's belongings, but it is much easier if they stay within the family or with close friends you can visit.

Each of us four siblings has something of Jeb's, our "Jeb Preservers." Mom has Jeb's favorite striped shirt, which she says she wears when she needs a "Jeb hug." My parents also have a gift from the Navy: a ceremonial folded American flag and bullet shells from the twenty-one-gun salute. I don't remember how we decided who would get what. In the end, it all felt OK because we could visit each other's "Jeb Preservers."

These days, I like to keep a few of Jeb's things around my house: his blue jacket, his Navy name tag, his Navy sweats, photos, and two postcards with his boyish handwriting on them. They are comforting now.

Seeing and touching these things, especially his handwriting, feels good. It connects us. It makes him real. It is tangible proof to me that he was really here.

One thing I wish I had is a recording of his voice. I can barely remember it. It would be wonderful to hear it—maybe sad, but comforting—because it would help me feel closer to him. Keep your recordings.

Every year after

Every year on March 21, I tell myself that I will visit the Navy's memorial at Moffett Field. The memorial is a large black granite slab that honors all twenty-seven crew members who died in the crash. Each young man has their named carved into the stone. Sometimes I need to let my fingers trace the inside of the deeply carved letters of Jeb's name to reassure myself he was real, this horrible accident really happened, I did have a little brother, and I remember him enough to miss him.

Some years I don't end up visiting the memorial. Sometimes I don't feel like being sad. Sometimes I'd rather celebrate Jeb's life by doing something he and I would enjoy, like hiking in the hills near Stanford or eating chocolate chip cookie dough while watching a silly movie.

When I do visit, I always bring Jeb early-blooming lilies from our garden and place them at the base of the etched names. Sometimes I cry, sometimes

I can't cry until I get home and hug my family, and sometimes I can't cry at all. I just feel quiet.

I've learned there are no rules. We need to allow ourselves to remember our loved ones in whatever way feels right for us.

Rituals

Jeb loved Halloween—especially the chocolate. Each year, in memory of Jeb and in celebration of Halloween and Mexico's Día de los Muertos, we set up an *ofrenda* in our dining nook. Along with glowing candles, orange marigolds, and fuschia flowers, we put up a few favorite photos, his old soccer ball, a little pumpkin, lots of Halloween candy, a bottle of beer, and his official US Navy name tag.

Getting to celebrate, honor, and miss him all at the same time truly feels good. And it's a healthy way to grieve. I recommend it.

Realizations

Jeb's age is frozen in time. A handsome photo of him in his flight suit hangs in our hallway. Over the past twenty-eight years, I've probably passed it a million times, but I'm just now realizing that he has never aged. He never got gray hair, or wrinkles, or gained weight around his middle. He will always be twenty-six years old with six-pack abs, wearing his *Top Gun* flight suit and a big wide grin.

Sometimes I look at his photo and catch myself wondering who that guy is—which is crazy. I used to not be able to look at his belongings, photos of him, or his handwriting without falling apart—especially if I wasn't expecting to see them. Now I look at his photo and feel sad that I can't *feel* more.

I've learned time may ease our pain, but it can also make it harder to remember. That brings its own form of grief.

Time

I've learned everyone heals at their own pace. For me, healing took more time than I expected. The first six months were the hardest. Sadness ebbed and flowed. Life was a blur. It didn't always make sense. I've learned you shouldn't let anyone tell you that you should be "over it by now."

Over the years, the wound in my heart has been torn open and healed shut so many times, and the scar has grown thicker with each healing. It's almost like the scar tissue has created distance between my heart and brain. In the first year after his death, my grief felt unbearable. The wound in my heart was huge. I desperately wanted my heart to stop feeling. Now, after so many years, it's really difficult to feel intense sadness around Jeb—to reopen the wound and reexperience his loss. I know that the wound in my heart is still deep, but it's far away, protected under comforting layers of healing scar tissue.

Twenty-five years later

On the twenty-fifth anniversary of the crash, in 2016, I attended the Navy's memorial service at Moffett Field. It felt good to catch up with Jeb's former colleagues and friends, tour the airplanes, and sit at his station on the plane. It never occurred to me that I might cry at the ceremony. It had been twenty-five years! Then somebody said something—I don't remember what—that opened up the old wound, and I couldn't stop the tears. But it felt good.

I've learned tears can change—from agonizing tears of despair to sweet tears. Happy-to-remember tears.

Why

Why did Jeb have to be in the airplane that crashed? Why did he have to die so young? Why did I have to beg him not to move to Hawaii? Why?

I've learned it's normal to ask why and equally normal to never know.

I don't know why Jeb was in that terrible accident. But I do know that I am happy and lucky that I got to know him, love him, and enjoy him. He was a gift. A one-of-a-kind, wonderfully fun, and inspiring gift.

What helped

- *Sleep. Sleep. Sleep.*

- *Long walks, especially under the comforting branches of wise old trees.*

- *Lying in bed, staring out the window, and thinking about him.*

- *Luxuriating in a hot bath.*

- *Wearing his way-too-big sweatpants.*

- *Sleeping with his soft, white duvet.*

- *Hugs.*

- *Listening to beautiful music.*

- *Buying beautiful flowers for my garden.*

- *Planting a beautiful tree in his memory.*

Planting a tree

I planted a six-inch redwood sapling in Jeb's memory. It is now sixty feet tall. It reminds me of him. Tall and thin. As it grows, it marks the passage of time. As memories of him drift away, his bigger-than-life spirit stays strong, rooted in my yard.

I've learned planting a tree sapling is a wonderful and natural way to honor a lost loved one. I wish I could give one to everyone I know who is grieving.

Staying busy

I've learned having a to-do list helps, especially in the first few weeks. It provided structure to my days and made me feel like I was accomplishing *something*. Some tasks helped my brain process the fact that he was really gone, like packing up his belongings, closing his accounts, and figuring out what to do with his car. Even though it was painful, having to tell different people over and over that I was calling because he had died helped me process the truth *and* helped me cry. I had no idea that the contacts I had to call would be as kind and compassionate as they were.

Staying busy, but not too busy, was tricky. I've learned if you try to avoid feeling sad by staying busy too much of the time, sadness and depression will creep up on you anyway, often unexpectedly and at inappropriate times. I still remember those painful moments and discomfiting situations, especially the ones that happened at work. Be patient with yourself. Grieving is hard.

Talking about him

I've learned you need to get up the courage to talk about your loved one more often, to ask friends to share stories about them. At one of the memorial services, I asked Jeb's friends and colleagues to tell me a funny Jeb story or share a fond memory. I recorded their stories on my phone. It hurt a little, but it was truly a relief to talk about him. He was such a goof! I would laugh and then tear up a bit. It felt good.

Pets

Grieving is such a lonely and isolating experience, and pets are healing. I wish I had had the comfort of our little dog, Butterscotch, when Jeb died. When I'm feeling down, Scotchy seems to know. She patiently lets me hug her warm, soft, and fuzzy self for as long as I want, and unlike many people, she doesn't feel the need to talk.

I've learned physical contact, such as a wordless hug or quietly holding someone's hand, is sometimes all we need. Don't be afraid to ask for what you want. Pets (and people) want to help.

Writing and drawing

So that I would never forget, I wrote and sketched images of some of my favorite memories of Jeb in a journal: teaching him to ski on tiny, yellow plastic skis in our backyard and sneaking candy in our tree fort. I also drew cartoons of fond summer memories, like Jeb flying off the rope swing into the lake, making giant campfires, catching fireflies, and playing "kick the can" after supper until it was too dark to see.

I've learned the more you record your memories—through sketching or writing—the more you're able to remember.

Drawing Jeb with his flight suit pockets bulging with chocolate candy led to drawing a headless chocolate Easter bunny. I remembered that every Easter, he would come to my house with a chocolate bunny and dare me to bite off its head. The drawings reminded me what a goof he was. I can still hear Jeb and our brothers doing hilarious imitations of the Three Stooges. I think it was Jeb's role in life to make us laugh.

I've learned you need to give yourself permission to express yourself, process your feelings, and share them with your loved ones. Whether it's writing, drawing, playing music, dancing, hiking, or whatever your interest may be, *doing* something physical may help you move through your grief.

Counseling

Grief counselors are incredibly helpful. The more I talked about what happened, the better I felt and the sooner I healed. If I hadn't finally asked for counseling and support, I couldn't have written this book. The pain of losing Jeb was so unbearable that it sent me into a long and deep depression. Going through the loss all alone, feeling so completely isolated, three thousand miles away from my family, and thinking that dealing with it all alone was my only option, was a painful mistake.

But I didn't know what I was doing, or supposed to be doing. I was just trying to get through each day. In retrospect, I wish I had belonged to a support group that understood what I was going through, but I didn't know there was such a thing.

I've learned you shouldn't isolate yourself. Try to find a support group or grief counselor. Surround yourself with people who understand and care, and will listen to you. You can find a highly credible list of national resources on Kara: https://kara-grief.org/resources/links

My niece

There must be some magical wavelength or connection out there. Eighteen years after the crash, my beautiful niece was born on March 21, 1999, at 2:27 a.m., the same date and exact time Jeb died. I lost a brother and got a niece on the same day.

I've learned it all comes full circle and the universe can offer up comforting surprises, like my niece in 1999, and six years later, my son.

My son

Now I have my own little boy named Charlie.
Sometimes I find myself calling him Jeb. Maybe it's
because they're both hilarious or because they both
have blond hair and big eyes. Maybe it's because
they share a bunk bed in my heart.

One of the few things that still makes me cry is that Jeb never got to meet my son. I wish Jeb was able to hold and cuddle Charlie, to go down the slide with him, to play with LEGOs, to build a contraption out of scrap wood and float it on the lake, to read to him, and to carry him high up on his shoulders, the way Jeb carried his other nephews.

Jeb would have been an awesome uncle to my son; he was just a big kid himself. A big, tall goofball.

I have to remind myself that I haven't finished processing this part of my grief yet. And that's OK. I know that it will happen with time.

My parents

———

My parents are proof that it will be OK. Life was, at times, unbearable for my parents. I'm sure they wondered if they could survive losing their youngest child. My heart breaks thinking about what they went through, especially now that I have a child. But my parents made it through. They even had a memorial bench built for Jeb at Veterans Memorial Park in our hometown in Maine. And my mom is now a proud member of the American Gold Star Mothers: She comforts other mothers who have lost children in the military, travels to Arlington Cemetery to place wreaths at Christmas, and waves from a white convertible driven by my eighty-nine-year-old dad (wearing his cool aviator sunglasses and American Legion hat) in their local Memorial Day parade.

They have found ways to honor Jeb in their own lives.

Hope

I try to live in honor of my brother. I fill my life with adventure, fun, beauty, family, and friends. I work hard. I want Jeb to be proud of me. I've changed the trajectory of my life several times because of the loss I experienced. His death at age twenty-six reminded me that life is short and I need to do what I am really passionate about. I asked Jeb for his advice, then decided to open my own design agency, which eventually became successful and enabled me to travel to far corners of the world. These trips were life altering and helped define my values. Thank you, Jeb.

When I turned forty-five in 2005, my life changed dramatically. I had a surprise baby boy, Charlie. Then in 2008, there was a massive downturn in the economy. Jeb was my inspiration to use this opportunity to seriously pursue a new career.

I asked Jeb—my constant reminder that life is fragile—what I should try next. I wanted to do something that would make him proud, something that really mattered, something that had always been a big dream of mine: working with underprivileged and immigrant children.

For the last eight years, I have been developing and teaching a design program to kids in a significantly underserved local school district. My program brings joy and imagination to learning. I've never felt so fulfilled.

I've learned, even after they are gone, our loved ones can still speak to us and guide us in life. In many ways, they can be our truest compass.

I hope Jeb would be proud of me.

Take care

Finally, take good care of yourself. Major trauma often makes people prone to illness or accidents. Five months after Jeb died, I got a virus I couldn't kick. I slept and slept. I think it was my body's way of telling me to stop—to let myself rest.

I hope my little book helps you rest and heal.

This little book
is a hug, from
me to you